Good Question!

How Does the Ear Hear?
AND OTHER QUESTIONS ABOUT . . .
The Five Senses

STERLING CHILDREN'S BOOKS
New York

STERLING CHILDREN'S BOOKS
New York

An Imprint of Sterling Publishing
387 Park Avenue South
New York, NY 10016

ISBN 978-1-4549-0672-8 (hardcover)
ISBN 978-1-4549-0673-5 (paperback)

Library of Congress Cataloging-in-Publication Data

Stewart, Melissa.
 How does the ear hear? : and other questions about the five senses /
Melissa Stewart ; art by Jim Madsen.
    pages cm. -- (Good question!)
 ISBN 978-1-4549-0672-8 (hardback) ISBN 978-1-4599-0673-5 (paperback)
1. Senses and sensation--Miscellanea--Juvenile literature. I. Title.
QP434.S7465 2014
612.8--dc23
                                                                                            2013026913

Distributed in Canada by Sterling Publishing
c/o Canadian Manda Group, 165 Dufferin Street
Toronto, Ontario, Canada M6K 3H6
Distributed in the United Kingdom by GMC Distribution Services
Castle Place, 166 High Street, Lewes, East Sussex, England BN7 1XU
Distributed in Australia by Capricorn Link (Australia) Pty. Ltd.
P.O. Box 704, Windsor, NSW 2756, Australia

Design by Andrea Miller
Art by Jim Madsen

For information about custom editions, special sales, and premium and corporate purchases, please contact Sterling Special Sales
at 800-805-5489 or specialsales@sterlingpublishing.com.

Manufactured in China
Lot #:
2 4 6 8 10 9 7 5 3 1
10/13

www.sterlingpublishing.com/kids

CONTENTS

How do your senses keep you safe?

Did you ever drink spoiled milk? Yuck! You probably spit it right out. And it's a good thing, too. Rotten milk can make you sick. Thank goodness your sense of taste helps you stay safe.

Taste is one of the five senses you depend on every day. Seeing, hearing, smelling, touching, and tasting help you understand the world. They can make your life better and they protect you from danger.

When your eyes see a friend, you feel happy. And when you spot a speeding car, you get out of the way. Your ears can hear a bird's sweet song and the blare of an alarm. Your nose smells the lovely scent of flowers and the stench of burning toast. Your skin can feel a hug or remind you to wear a coat on cold days. And your tongue does more than warn you when milk has spoiled. It also savors the taste of chocolate chip cookies.

How do messages from your senses travel to your brain?

Your eyes, ears, nose, skin, and tongue sense the world around you. But your body can't react until your brain gets the message. And that takes nerves—long, stringy bundles of cells. The 30,000 miles of nerves snaking through your body carry messages to your brain at 150 miles per hour. After your brain processes the information, it sends out more messages. They race along your nerves at speeds as great as 200 miles per hour.

SIGHT

HEARING

TOUCH

TASTE

SMELL

The Human Eye

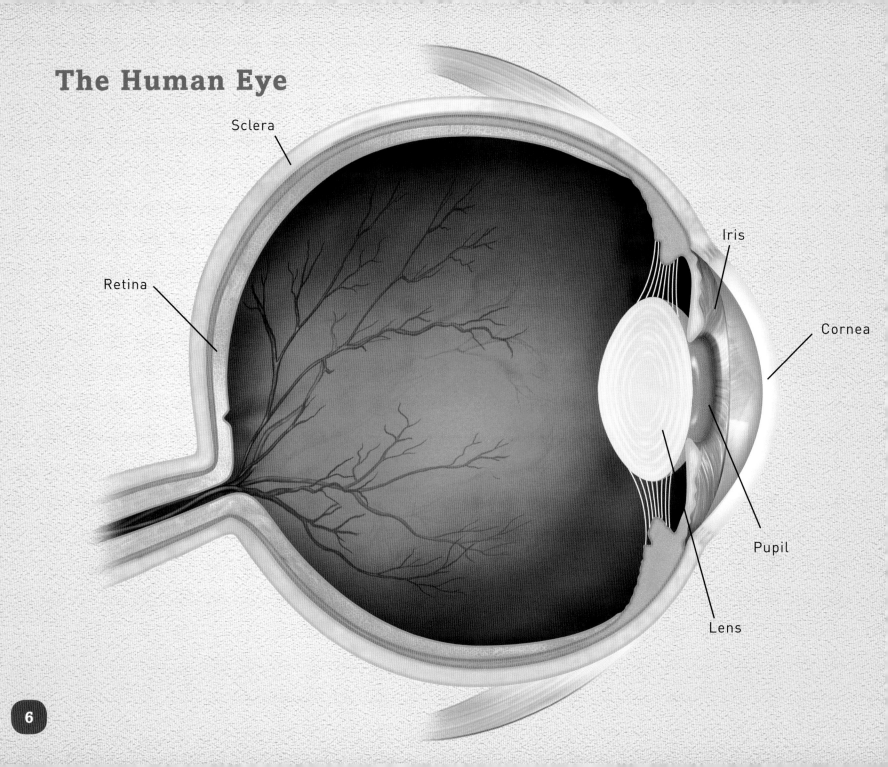

Sclera

Retina

Iris

Cornea

Pupil

Lens

How do your eyes work?

Even though you have five senses, your eyes take in 80 percent of the information you use to understand the world. That makes them very important.

When you look at an eyeball, you see a colorful iris surrounded by white sclera. The tiny black spot in the center, the pupil, is a hole that lets light into your eye. What you don't see is the cornea, a clear window that covers the front of the eye.

Muscles in the iris control the amount of light that whizzes through your pupil and hits your lens. When muscles attached to your lens stretch, nearby objects come into focus on your retina. That's how you see the pages of this book. When the muscles attached to your lens relax, distant objects—like an airplane in the sky—look crystal clear.

Millions of light-sensing cells, or sensors, cover your retina. They capture light rays and turn them into messages that travel to your brain. Then your brain processes the information and tells your body how to react.

Why do some people wear eyeglasses?

If a person's cornea isn't the right shape, objects look blurry. If an eyeball is too short or too long, some objects are hard to see. Luckily, eyeglasses can solve these problems. Eyeglass lenses redirect light and focus it correctly on the retina.

Why are two eyes better than one?

Even though your eyes are close together, each one sees the world a little bit differently. That comes in handy when you want to pick an apple or catch a baseball.

Ever tried playing catch with one eye closed? It's not easy. Everything looks flat, which makes it harder to tell how far away the ball is.

But when both eyes are open, your brain gets information from two sources. It combines the two images to create a 3-D view of the world. You know exactly how far away the ball is—and where you should put your hands to catch it.

Why do some animals have eyes on the sides of their heads?

Think of it this way: *Eyes to the front, they hunt. Eyes to the side, they hide.*

Wolves, eagles, lions, tigers—they're some of the fiercest hunters on Earth. They all have eyes on the front of their heads just like you. Seeing the world in 3-D helps them catch prey.

Deer, rabbits, chipmunks, and chickadees lead a different kind of life. They are always on the lookout for danger. Because their eyes are on the sides of their heads they can see far to the right and left while they eat. That makes it hard for enemies to sneak up on them.

Look at the location of the eyes on these animals.
Which animals are predators? Which are prey?

The eyes on this land snail are on the tips of its long tentacles. The little critter moves its tentacles up and down and from side to side to get the best possible view of its surroundings.

Do all animals see the way people do?

No way!

Most spiders have eight eyes, but that doesn't mean they see four times better than we do. Their simple eyes can sense light and darkness, but they can't see objects. Snails, sea jellies, and sea stars have simple eyes too.

Many insects, lobsters, and crabs have huge eyes with lots of little lenses. They can see right and left and up and down, all at the same time. And they can spot even the slightest movement.

Plenty of animals don't see colors the way we do. Some monkeys can't see red. Many insects see only yellow and blue, and dogs mostly see the world as yellow, blue, and gray. All birds and some insects see colors people can't see.

Lions, leopards, cougars, and cheetahs all hunt at night. How do these cats see so well in the dark? A mirrorlike structure in their eyes collects light and then reflects it. This magnifies the small amount of light available, making it easier for them to see at night.

Whirligig beetles and four-eyed fish can watch what's happening above and below the water at the same time. What's their secret? Their eyeballs are split in half. The tops can see in air, while the bottoms work best underwater.

Why are two ears better than one?

To find out, try this: Cover one ear with your hand, shut your eyes, and listen. What do you hear? Can you guess where the sounds are coming from? Probably not.

Now try listening with both ears. When your ears work together, it's a lot easier to pinpoint the source of a sound. If the honking of a car horn sounds louder in your left ear, your brain lets you know the angry driver is in a car to your left. To get out of the way, you should move to the right.

Why do your ears stick out?

When you throw a pebble into a pond, you see tiny waves ripple out in every direction. Something similar happens when a bell rings or your teacher talks or a car horn blasts. Invisible waves of sound ripple through the air.

The air all around you is full of sound waves, but you only hear a noise when the waves enter your ears. Because your pinnas, or outer ears, stick out of your head, lots of sound waves bump into them. Your pinnas collect the sounds and funnel them into your ear canals.

The Human Ear

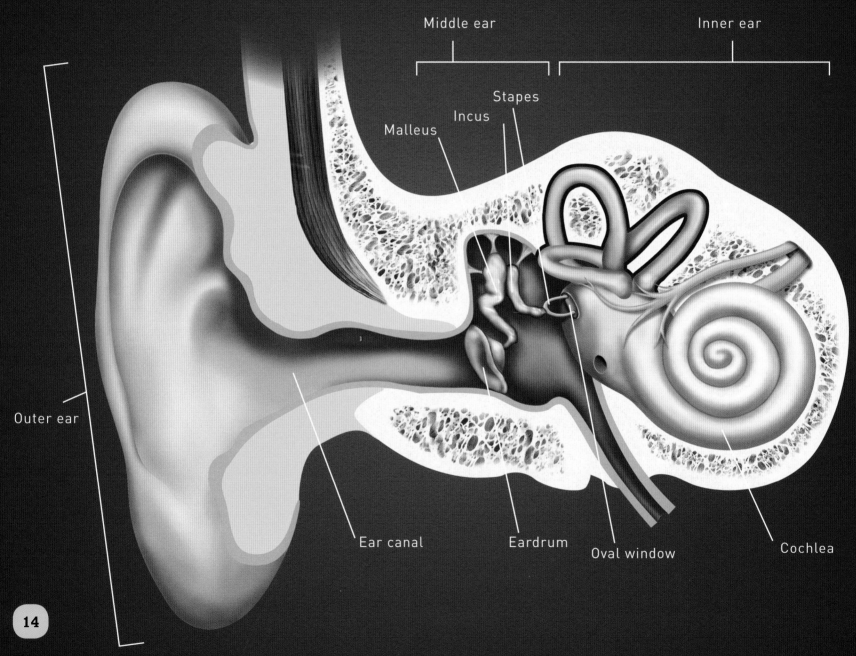

Middle ear

Inner ear

Stapes

Incus

Malleus

Outer ear

Ear canal

Eardrum

Oval window

Cochlea

How does the ear hear?

When you look at the opening to your ear canal, it's hard to imagine what's inside. That dark little tunnel inside each ear is about half as long as your pinky finger. At the far end, sound waves crash into your eardrum—a thin, tightly stretched membrane that separates your outer ear from your middle ear.

Crashing sound waves make your eardrum vibrate, and that back-and-forth motion causes three tiny bones inside your middle ear to shake. The vibrations move through your malleus bone first, then your incus, and finally your stapes—the smallest bone in your body. Your stapes jiggles your oval window—a membrane that separates your middle ear from your inner ear.

Each time your oval window bulges forward, it pushes against fluid inside your snail-shaped cochlea. And that motion forms a new wave. As waves of fluid roll through the cochlea, they shake a tiny structure called the organ of Corti. More than twenty thousand hearing sensors inside the organ of Corti detect the vibrations and turn them into messages that travel to your brain. Then your brain quickly processes the information it receives from both ears and sends out more messages that tell your body how to react.

Why does a fire alarm sound louder than a whisper?

If you've watched crashing ocean waves, you know that some are bigger than others. Sound waves come in different sizes, too. Airplanes and fire alarms create big, tall sound waves. But whispers and purring cats produce small, short sound waves. The taller a sound wave is, the louder it sounds.

Scientists measure the loudness of a sound in decibels (dB). People can hear sounds as soft as 1 dB. If something is louder than 150 dB, you will feel pain in your ears.

Can some animals hear sounds that people can't?

They sure can. Here's why: Some sound waves are long and wide. They hit your ears more slowly than waves that are close together. Long sound waves create low-pitched noises like the rumble of distant thunder. Closely spaced sound waves create high-pitched noises like the screech of car breaks.

Scientists measure pitch in hertz (Hz). Most kids can hear sounds with pitches between 20 and 20,000 Hz. But many animals can hear sounds outside that range. Elephant, whales, and fish can hear very low-pitched sounds. Horses and dogs can hear very high-pitched sounds.

Elephants, alligators, whales, giraffes, hippos, rhinos, and even some birds can communicate by using low-pitched sounds people can't hear. Dolphins, bats, rats, and mice use sounds with pitches as high as 150,000 Hz to talk to one another.

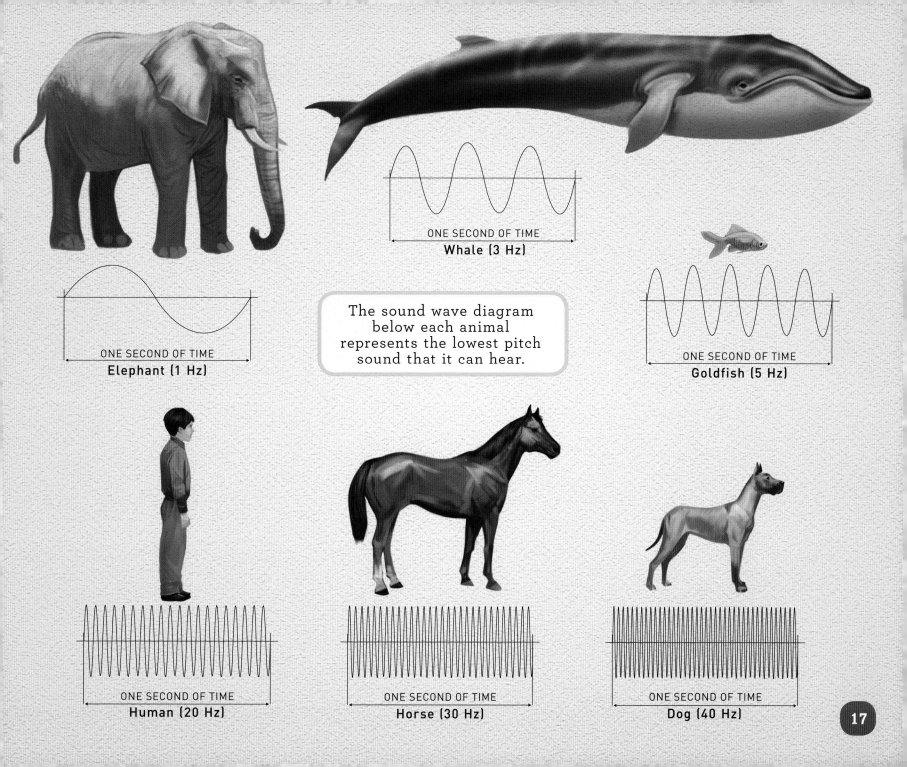

ONE SECOND OF TIME
Whale (3 Hz)

ONE SECOND OF TIME
Elephant (1 Hz)

The sound wave diagram below each animal represents the lowest pitch sound that it can hear.

ONE SECOND OF TIME
Goldfish (5 Hz)

ONE SECOND OF TIME
Human (20 Hz)

ONE SECOND OF TIME
Horse (30 Hz)

ONE SECOND OF TIME
Dog (40 Hz)

The Human Nose

Brain

As air (blue arrows) moves through your nose, only a small amount passes over the area where smelling occurs (box). A magnified view of that area shows the scent sensors that detect odors.

Nasal cavity

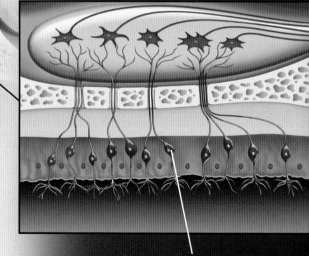

Scent sensors

How does breathing help you smell?

Close your eyes and take a deep breath. The 2,300 gallons of air you breathe every day is full of things you might not expect—dust, dirt, pollen, germs, and even little bugs. It also contains millions of tiny scent molecules.

Most of the air you inhale races down your throat and into your lungs. But about 2 percent of it takes a different path. It travels up to the top of your nose and passes over the area where smelling occurs. The postage stamp–size patch of tissue is packed with about 5 million scent sensors.

When scent molecules bump into tiny hairs hanging down from your scent sensors, messages travel to your brain. As soon as your brain processes the information, it lets the rest of your body know how to react.

How many scents can people smell?

Most people can smell between three thousand and ten thousand different odors. Women and children can usually detect more scents than men.

People don't always agree on what smells good and what smells bad. Many people feel sick to their stomach when they smell a skunk's spray, but some people aren't bothered by the odor.

Do some animals have a better sense of smell than people?

f you have a pet dog or cat, you probably know the answer to this question. Yes! For many animals, having a strong sense of smell is a matter of life and death.

- A rabbit has ten times more scent sensors than people do. And it's a good thing, too. The cute, cuddly critter depends on its nose to sniff out food and pick up the scent of enemies.
- An anteater's nose is forty times more powerful than yours. It can catch a whiff of ants and termites from several miles away.
- A vulture can pick up the scent of a dead, rotting animal from high in the sky. Then it circles lower and lower until it zeroes in on its meal.
- A polar bear has one of the world's best noses. It can pick up the scent of a dead seal from twenty miles away.
- Some dogs have about a billion scent sensors inside their noses. That's why police officers can train them to search for missing people and to sniff out bombs and illegal drugs.

The best basketball players know that their sensitive fingertips can help them win a game.

Are some parts of your skin more sensitive than others?

Rub the tips of your fingers on a sheet of paper. Now rub your elbow on the same piece of paper. Why can you feel the paper better with your fingers? Because your fingers are more sensitive to touch.

To find out which other parts of your body are super sensitive to touch, try this: Put on a blindfold or shut your eyes. Ask a friend to press the tips of a pair of tweezers gently on different parts of your body. Try your hands, lips, nose, neck, arms, shoulders, legs, back, feet, and toes.

Make a list of places on your body where you could feel both tips of the tweezers. Next, make a second list of places where you could only feel one tip.

What you'll probably find is that your hands, lips, nose, neck, feet, and toes are more sensitive than your arms, legs, and shoulders. The middle of your back is the least sensitive part of your body.

The Human Skin

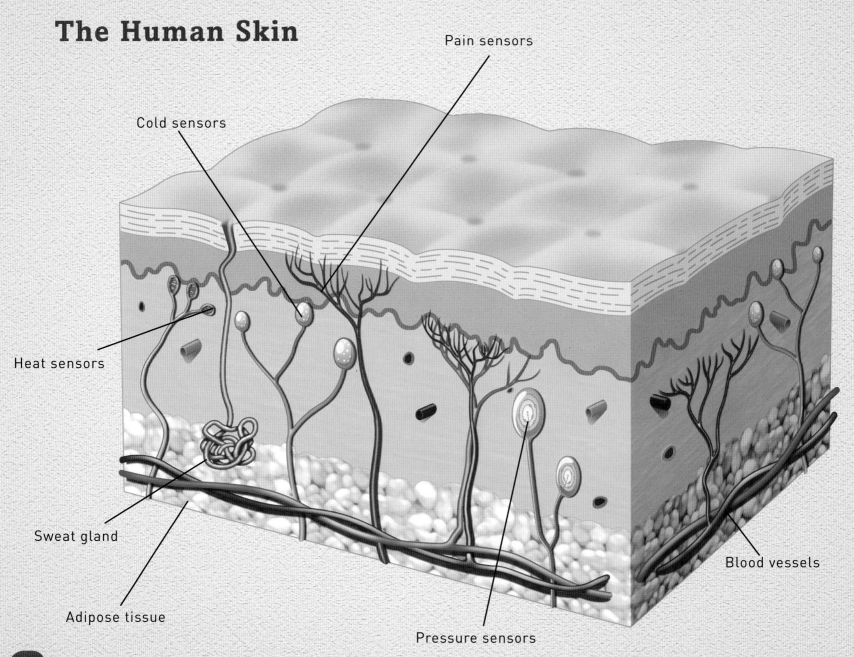

Pain sensors

Cold sensors

Heat sensors

Sweat gland

Adipose tissue

Pressure sensors

Blood vessels

Why are your fingers so sensitive?

The skin on your fingers has more pressure sensors than any other part of your body, so your fingertips can feel even the slightest touch. All those pressure sensors make it easier to pick up a small object like a pea. They also help you hold onto delicate objects, like a flower petal. Pressure sensors can sense textures, too, so they let you know that a sock is softer than a rock.

Why do ice cubes feel cold?

When you touch an ice cube, the pressure sensors in your fingertips send messages to your brain. That's how you know that ice is hard and smooth. But those aren't the first things you notice when you touch ice. That's because your skin also has three other kinds of sensors—pain sensors, heat sensors, and cold sensors. Temperature messages travel faster than pressure messages, so your brain screams, "COLD!" when you touch ice.

Pain sensors are simple structures, so they collect information quickly, and their messages travel to your brain even faster than information about temperature. Why is that so important? Because if your fingers—or any other parts of your body are in pain—your brain needs to know right away. By working together, your touch sensors and your brain get you out of dangerous situations as quickly as possible.

What causes an itch?

Plenty of things can make you itch—head lice, insect bites, sunburn, and clothing tags. But lots of times, there's no explanation for that prickly feeling. These mysterious itches have scientists stumped.

What scientists do know is that as soon as an itch message reaches you brain, you start to scratch. And that gets the attention of your pain sensors. While your mind focuses on the mild pain of scraping fingernails, blood rushes to the site of the itch. After that, it doesn't take long for the annoying itch to fade away.

Why can't you tickle yourself?

A gentle tickle can make anyone wriggle and squirm. That's because light, playful touch drives your pressure sensors crazy. But have you ever noticed that you can't tickle yourself?

The pressure sensors in your skin send out messages along your nerves no matter who does the tickling. But if your brain knows what's coming, it ignores the input. It doesn't send out messages that tell your voice to giggle and your muscles to pull away.

How does saliva help you taste?

To find out, try this: Stick out your tongue and dry off the tip with a napkin. Then sprinkle a little bit of sugar on it. What do you taste?

Now pull your tongue back into your mouth and swish it around in spit, or saliva. Put a little bit more sugar on your tongue. Do you taste the difference? You should. The taste buds on your tongue can't do their job until saliva starts to digest, or break down, food into smaller bits.

Why does food taste different when you have a cold?

Most people have about ten thousand taste buds on their tongue. And each one has sensors that can detect five different flavors—sweet, salty, sour, bitter, and a rich, meaty flavor called umami.

All the other food flavors you enjoy come from how they smell—not how they taste. Scent molecules from food float up the back of your throat and into your nose. When they bump into scent sensors, messages race to your brain, and you catch a whiff of your meal.

When you have a cold, your nose gets all stuffed up. Since scent molecules can't drift up to the scent sensors at the top of your nose, food doesn't "taste" nearly as good.

Thank goodness our senses work most of the time!

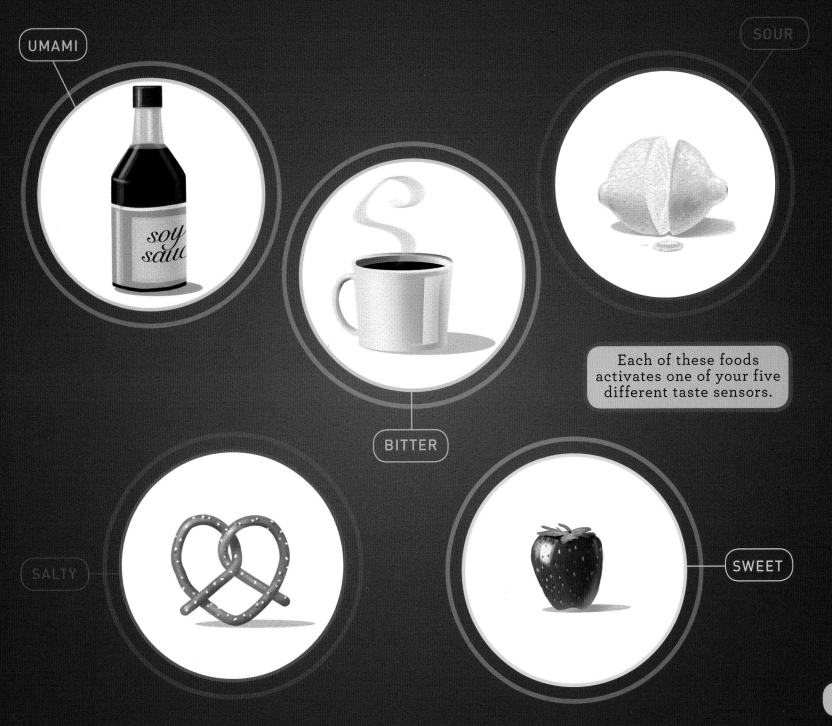

UMAMI

SOUR

BITTER

Each of these foods activates one of your five different taste sensors.

SALTY

SWEET

29

Books to Read

Seuling, Barbara. *Your Skin Weighs More than Your Brain: And Other Freaky Facts About Your Skin, Skeleton, and Other Body Parts*. Minneapolis, MN: Picture Window Books, 2007.

Stewart, Melissa. *The Eyes Have It: The Secrets of Eyes and Seeing*. Tarrytown, NY: Marshall Cavendish/Benchmark Books, 2009.

Stewart, Melissa. *Now Hear This: The Secrets of Ears and Hearing*. Tarrytown, NY: Marshall Cavendish/Benchmark Books, 2009.

Stewart, Melissa. *Up Your Nose: The Secrets of Schnozes and Snouts*. Tarrytown, NY: Marshall Cavendish/Benchmark Books, 2009.

Stewart, Melissa. *The Skin You're In: The Secrets of Skin*. Tarrytown, NY: Marshall Cavendish/ Benchmark Books, 2010.

Stewart, Melissa. *You've Got Nerve! The Secrets of the Brains and Nerves*. Tarrytown, NY: Marshall Cavendish/Benchmark Books, 2010.

Websites to Visit

GET BODY SMART: THE NOSE
www.getbodysmart.com/ap/respiratorysystem/nose/nasalmucosa/tutorial.html

KIDS HEALTH
kidshealth.org/kid/

NEUROSCIENCE FOR KIDS
faculty.washington.edu/chudler/introb.html

THE SOUND SITE
www.smm.org/sound/nocss/top.html

THAT EXPLAINS IT!
www.coolquiz.com/trivia/explain/

For bibliography and free activities visit: www.sterlingpublishing.com/kids/good-question

INDEX